Fish-it5

Published by:
Arc Publishing and Print
166 Knowle Lane
Sheffield S11 9SJ
07809 172872

Produced By: Chris Keeling

Whilst every effort has been made to ensure the contents of this
publication are accurate at the time of publishing.
Arc Publishing and Print and those involved in producing the content
of "Fish-It 5 North Yorkshire" cannot be held responsible for any
errors, omissions or changes in the details of this guide or for the
consequences of any reliance on the information provided in it. We
have tried to ensure accuracy in this guide but things do change and
we would be grateful if readers could advise us of any inaccuracies
they have found.

ISBN: 978-1-906722-09-8

ACKNOWLEDGEMENTS
I would like to thank the following for their
help in producing this guide:
Bradford No1 Angling Association.
Jim Steele for venue information.

All fishery owners and angling clubs who have kindly
provided information and to those that gave permission to
use images from their websites.

May 2009

Arc Publishing and Print
166 Knowle Lane
Sheffield
S11 9SJ

C O N T E N T S

W E L C O M E

Welcome to Fish-it 5 (North Yorkshire). Like many other anglers, my time on the bank is limited, but I like to grab a few hours fishing whenever and wherever I can. As in my previous books, I have tried to provide a mixed selection of venues to entice you to try a new fishery. There is plenty of information, along with photos of most venues, so hopefully you will find the ideal water to suit your method of fishing.

I hope I have produced a book that gives a good idea of what a fishing venue has to offer before setting out on a lengthy journey, only to be disappointed when you reach your destination.

I have enjoyed fishing many of these fisheries, but not all. Information has been supplied to me from anglers and fishery owners from the area and I would like to thank them for their support.

If you have details of a venue and you would like it included in a future publication, please fill in the form at the back of this guide.

I hope you find this book useful and wish you good luck, good fishing and remember -

"A bad day's fishing is still better than a good day's work!"

Chris Keeling

I have tried to ensure the accuracy of this guide but things do change very quickly so if you know of any inaccuracies or any fisheries I have not included I would be grateful if you could fill out and return the form at the back of the guide.

GETTING STARTED

Fishing is enjoyed by many people as both a sport and a hobby. Basically anglers can be divided into three types.

Firstly the **pleasure angler** who fishes just for the relaxation and fun - enjoying their surroundings but unworried about the number of fish caught (as long as they get a few).

The match angler is competitive and has a wide knowledge of the sport. He enjoys competing against other anglers and has an impressive collection of tackle which enables him to fish large lakes, small ponds, canals and rivers.

The specimen angler or hunter is a loner, usually intent on catching a large fish. Most specialise in a particular species - eg. carp, pike, barbel.

The specimen carp hunter can spend thousands on his tackle and many hours making special rigs in his bid to catch that really big fish.

Most people, however, take up fishing purely for pleasure.

To get started you will need the following:-

Rod: Most beginners start with a match rod. A good choice would be a 12' carbon fibre rod. Your local tackle shop will advise you, ask the assistant to fit a reel to the rod. It should be comfortable to hold and feel well balanced. Carbon composite rods are cheaper than the carbon rods. In the long run it pays to get a good carbon rod.

Reel: There is a wide range of reels. Again ask for advice from the tackle shop or try one of the many angling forums on the internet. You will get sound advice from more experienced anglers. Begin with a fixed spool reel which will cost you between £15 and £25. Most fixed reels come with two spools. Put 3lb line on one and a heavier line (6lb) on the other for catching larger fish.

Keepnet: Ideal if you like to see your catch when you've finished fishing. Make sure you get a large net and fully open it whilst in the water - this allows the fish room to move. Make sure it is at least 8' in length. They are made in either round or rectangular shape. Some have adjustable legs for use on sloping banks. Note, many fisheries don't allow keepnets except in matches. Check fishery rules.

Landing Net: This is a vital piece of equipment for landing a hooked fish. Again there are various sizes available. Don't buy one too small or you will have a problem landing that unexpected big carp! Never attempt to swing fish to hand, get into the habit of landing all fish no matter how small. Swinging in larger fish will damage the fish and could also break your rod.

Floats: There are many types of float to chose from, but wagglers are the most popular. The best way to attach them to your line is by fixing a float adaptor, this is a piece of silicon tubing with a swivel eye, which allows the float to be changed without breaking down the rest of your tackle. Most floats are made of plastic, balsa or peacock quill. For faster flowing waters many anglers use stick floats.

Seatbox: This is useful, not only as a seat but as a storage place for your fishing gear. The Shakespeare seatbox is very popular. It is made of light weight plastic with good storage space and two detachable trays - ideal for the beginner. More expensive boxes have hinged lids and separate storage compartments for rigs, plus adjustable legs for use on uneven ground.

Line: The line is a thin string made from a single fibre, this is called monofilament line. It comes in different colours but clear is the commonly used type. Monofilament degrades with time and can weaken when exposed to heat and sunlight. When stored on a spool for a long time, it may come off the fishing reel in coils or loops. It is advisable to change monofilament line at regular intervals to prevent degradation. Load your reel with 3 to 4lb. line for float fishing. If you targeting heavier fish then use 6 to 8lb. line.

Hooks: There is an enormous variety of fish hooks that will be on display at your local tackle shop. Buy hooks that are already tied to a nylon hook length and make sure you get barbless ones as they are much easier to remove from the fish. Size 22 (small) are ideal for small roach and perch, upto size 14 for larger fish.

Rodrests: These attach to a bankstick which is a pointed metal stick with a universal threaded end. There are many types of rests, just chose one that will support your rod comfortably.

Shot: Shot comes in sizes SSG to No.8 and can be bought separately or in multi-size shot dispensers. The bigger shot is used to fix your waggler at the correct depth position on your line. The lighter smaller shot is used to sink your line and set the appearance of your float on the water surface.

Plummet: A plummet is a weight which is used to accurately measure the depth of water you are going to fish. They are attached to your hook. If the float disappears after you have cast in, then you are set too shallow and need to move your float up the line.

Disgorger: This is used to safely remove the hook from the mouth of a fish. The plastic barrel type are best. Simply slide the disgorger down the line until contact is made with the hook bend. Give it a slight push and out will come the hook.

Fishing Licence: Anyone over the age of 12 will need an Environment Agency Rod Licence. This allows you to fish for coarse fish but you will also require permission from the owner of the fishing rights. You can get this either by club membership or by purchasing a day ticket. Rod licences run for twelve months beginning on 31st. March. Eight day and one day licences are also available. You can these from post offices or on line @ environment-agency.gov.uk/fish.
Adult licences cost £26.00 for a full year.
8 day licences are £9.50
1 day licences are £3.50
Junior (12-16 years) are only £5.00
Concessionary licences for people aged
65 or over are £17.25
(Check the Environment Agency web site for the latest prices)

In the cooler months you will need warm and waterproof clothing. An umbrella is also a good idea - get one that tilts. There are a few rules to keep everyone happy. Close all gates. Have respect for the landowner who has given permission for you to use his land and most importantly don't leave litter - especially discarded line and hooks.

Good fishing!

P O L E   F I S H I N G
F O R   T H E   B E G I N N E R

Of all the different methods of fishing I've tried, I haven't found any of them as accurate or as easy as pole fishing. To be able to place your bait and feed to the exact spot, sometimes only inches from an island or group of reeds is what makes pole fishing so productive and fun.

T A C K L E   N E E D E D

A Pole

Poles come in various sizes, from 4 metres (usually called a whip) to poles of 18.5 metres. They also vary dramatically in price as well, this is usually governed by weight and rigidity. The lighter and straighter (no droop at the end) the more expensive they are. I recommend a pole between 11 and 13 metres, stay away from the smaller telescopic ones. Many tackle shops have poles ready assembled for you to handle, make sure you are comfortable with its weight and it feels well balanced. Test that it takes apart smoothly. If possible, get a pole with a spare top section as they enable you to rig up for different species and size of fish.

Pole Rigs

Experienced anglers can make up their own pole rigs but beginners are advised to buy ready-made. There are plenty of quality ready made rigs available for as little as £2.99. These rigs come with a main line with a loop on the end (used to attach the line to the stonfo connector at the tip of your pole). A float with enough shot below it to cock it nicely in the water and a length of lower breaking strain line, which has a spade end hook tied to it. The float and shot can slide down the line and be adjusted accordingly.

Pole Elastic

The elastic that runs through the top sections of your pole cushions the fight of a hooked fish and allows you to play it. Elastics are graded in sizes 1-20.
The following list is a good guide for the beginner:
1. For small roach and perch for example - use a No4 elastic with a 1lb hook length and a 2lb main line.
2. If fishing for small carp and tench or skimmer bream use a No8 or 10 elastic with a 3.5lb main line and 2.5lb. hook length.
3. When fishing for carp up to 12lbs use a No.16 to 18 elastic, and a main line of 8lb with a 6.5lb hook length.

S T A R T   T O   F I S H

Fishing Position

Get your seatbox in position. Ideally, when sitting on the box, your thighs should be in a horizontal position, at right angles to your lower leg. Holding the pole correctly makes it comfortable for long periods and prevents backache. For a right handed person you need to rest the pole across your knees with your left hand supporting it. Put your right forearm along the end of the pole and firmly grip the pole with your right hand. Have close to hand - your bait, landing net, disgorger and anything else you may require for your days fishing. It is important to have your pole roller in the correct location. The pole has to be well balanced in your hands when it leaves the roller - this prevents rig tangles when shipping out.

Start Fishing

You have set up your pole and plumbed your depth - so now you are ready to fish. Make sure you have between 10" and 20" of line between the tip and float. In more windy conditions you may want to lengthen this. Feed your swim with groundbait (if allowed) plus a few bits of your hook bait. This is more accurately done using a pole cup which can be fixed to the end of your pole. Put your bait on the hook and ship out your pole trying to keep your rig in the water as this prevents tangles. Lay the rig on the water lengthways. The shot on the line will pull the line under the water and cock the float.
Enjoy your first pole fishing day!

A B O U T   T H I S   G U I D E

To help you locate a fishery, in the North Yorkshire area.
I have placed a float symbol with its location
number on the area map. See page 12

Each page contains details of a fishery,
with information on the following:

Ticket Price:
  Day ticket costs plus details on OAPs, disabled and junior concessions.

Directions:
  Usually from the nearest city or town, or from the closest motorway junction.

Description:
  A brief outline of what the fishery looks like plus details on features such as islands, depths and the best places to fish.

Types of Fish:
  List of species present, many with estimated weights.

Rules/Bans:
  The restrictions set by the fishery on type of baits, hooks etc.

Number of Lakes:
  The number of waters available to fish at the venue.

Facilities:
  What is available at each location i.e. cafe.

Telephone:
  The number of the owner, angling club secretary or match organiser.

Sat Nav:
  Post Codes for use on satellite navigation systems.

Blood Knot

This knot can be used to join two lines together, start by overlapping the ends of the two lines.

Twist one end round the other line four times and pass it between the two lines.

Do the same with the other end of line, making sure the previous step does not come undone.

Before pulling tight wet the knot to lubricate this also make it hold better. Trim off the two ends.

Pull on the loose end to tighten. Trim the line.

Half Blood Knot

Used mainly for joining hook to line.

Thread the end of your line through the eye of your hook.

Pass the free end underneath the line and bring it back over the line to form a loop

Continue to loop the free end over the line about four times.

Pass the loose end between the eye of the hook and the first loop.

Pull on the loose end to tighten. Trim the line.

Double Overhand loop

This knot is used to create a loop at the end of a line. Also known as the surgeon's loop.

To begin, double the end of the line back against itself.

Tie an overhand knot in the doubled line.

The doubled end should then be tucked through the loop again.

Pull the knot as tight as possible and trim of the end.

Water Knot

This knot can also be known as the surgeon's knot. It is useful for joining a lighter hook line to your mainline

Hold the ends of the two lines alongside each other so that they overlap by about six inches.

Take hold of the two lines and make a wide loop.

Holding the two lines together. Pass the ends of the line through the loop four times.

Pull the lines tightly so that the loop makes a knot. Trim the two ends.

SPECIES / SYMBOLS

Most commonly found in
the North Yorkshire area.

 BARBEL

 Camping

 BREAM

 Caravan Site

 **CARP**

 Drinks

 **CHUB**

 Disabled Access

 **CRUCIAN**

 Toilets

 **IDE**

 Food

 **ORFE**

 Parking

 **PERCH**

 EEL

 **PIKE**

 **GUDGEON**

 **ROACH**

 Location of fishery on Map

 **RUDD**

To help you find the nearest
place to get tackle and bait,
turn to page 61
for a list of tackle shops
in North Yorkshire

 **TENCH**

TROUT

11

North Yorkshire Venues

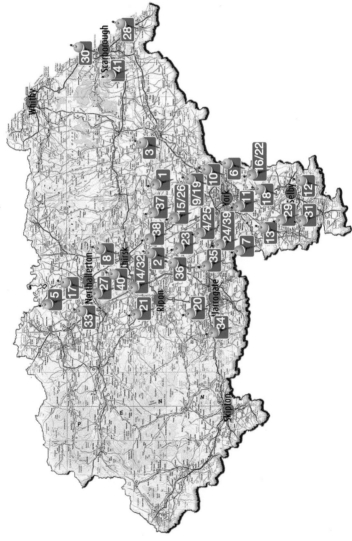

Birkdale Fishery
Mowthorpe Lane, Terrington.

Ticket Price: Day ticket £6.00 for 2rods. £4.00 Concessions.

Directions: Take the A64 from York and about 5 miles outside of Malton, turn left to Welburn. Go through Welburn and follow the signs for Ganthorpe, go through the village and at the next junction turn left towards Terrington. Once in Terrington turn onto Mowthorpe Lane. You will see the fishery as you go down the lane.

Description: This is a beautiful secluded fishery set in the Howardian Hills. There are three lakes to try, with main Lake being the largest at 4 acres, with depths between 4 and 11 feet. All three lakes have an island in, and this is where most fish are caught. Carp go to around 23lb, big enough for most anglers that come here. There is also a good stock of roach and bream that can make up some good summer bags.

Types of Fish: Stocked with carp to 23lb. Roach, bream, tench, barbel, rudd, chub and some trout

Rules/Bans: Barbless hooks only, night fishing allowed only with prior permission. No nuts, peas or beans. Groundbait in moderation only. Keepnets and landing nets must be dipped prior to fishing.

Facilities: **Number of Lakes:** Three

Sat Nav: YO60 6PZ   **Telephone:** 01653 648301   1

Brafferton Carp Fishery

Boroughbridge Road, Brafferton.

Ticket Price: Day ticket £6.00 (2 rods) Concessions £4.00
Purchased on the bank.

Directions: From York take the A19 and come off just after
Easingwold. This will be sign posted Raskelf. Go through
Raskelf and follow signs to Brafferton. You will find the lakes
in the village.

Description: Renowned for the carp fishing, this four lake
fishery is a must try venue. With around 200 pegs there is
always a peg to suite your method of fishing. Beware there
are some big fish here, so don't fish light. Ghost Lake as
the name suggests is stuffed with carp many over 20lbs.
Spring Lake has a good stock of silver fish as well as good
sized carp. F1 Lake is the match Lake. Most pegs are
suitable for the disabled angler and their is plenty of car
parking space.

Types of Fish: Stock includes: Ghost, common and mirror
carp. Roach, bream, tench, rudd and crucian carp.

Rules/Bans: Barbless hooks only.
Keepnets are allowed.

Facilities: **Number of Lakes:** Four

Sat Nav: YO61 2PD   **Telephone:** 01423 360402   2

Brickyard Farm Lakes

High St, Amotherby, Malton.

Ticket Price: Day tickets £7.00 Evening ticket £5.00
Weekly ticket £35.00 Additional rods £2.00 each.

Directions: Brickyard Farm Lakes is located in North
Yorkshire's beautiful Ryedale. Leave Malton on the B1257.
Go through Swinton and at the crossroad at Amotherby turn
right. You will find the lakes on your left.

Description: Brickyard Farm Lakes is a small friendly caravan
site with three lakes to try. Old Lake is more than one
hundred years old and contains a variety of coarse fish.
Abbie Lake was excavated in the early 1990's and has
matured well. Abbie contains carp, a good many being in
double figures. Jacob's Cut is the newest lake being
constructed for the millennium. The silver fish have become
established and good catches are reported all year round.

Types of Fish: Carp, bream, roach, perch and crucian carp.

Rules/Bans: Barbless hooks only. No keepnets.

Number of Lakes: Three

Facilities:

Sat Nav: YO17 6TL   **Telephone:** 01653 693606   3

Carpvale Ponds
Church Lane, Moor Monkton, York.

Ticket Price: Coarse Lakes £7.00. Concessions £5.00.

Directions: Follow the A59 from the A1 junction towards York. About two miles after crossing the River Nidd at Skip Bridge turn left at a sign indicating Moor Monkton village. Follow for about one mile and turn left at the sign for the fishery car park.

Description: This is a very basic straight forward quality fishery. There are three ponds, Cyprio, Match, and Front Pond, each one slightly different from the other. All have Islands to target, but the favoured spots seem to be the corners. Personally I prefer to fish the end of the island in Cyprio Pond as this has the larger carp and some huge tench to over 8lbs.

Types of Fish: Carp, tench, and bream are the main species, plus an assortment of silver fish.

Rules/Bans: Fishing is from 7am until sunset. Fishing is with one rod, line and hook only. No Keepnets allowed - except in a pre-booked match. No fish to be removed from the site. Anybody with litter in or around his/her peg will be asked to leave. Barbless or microbarb hooks only to be used. Fishing is only allowed from designated platforms. A current rod licence is required. No fish to be held in cloths or towels No braided or hook lengths.

Number of Lakes: Three

Facilities: 4

Telephone: 01904 738249   **Sat Nav:** YO26 8LA

Cornhill Farm Ponds

East Cowton, Northallerton.

Ticket Price: Day ticket £6.00. Concessions £4.00.
Afternoons after 4pm £4.00.

Directions: Take the A167 from Darlington to Northallerton.
You will pass the village of Dalton on the A167, after a mile
and a half turn right, onto the B1263 signed for Richmond.
Keep going on this road until you see the signs for the
fishery on the left hand side, just after the turn off for East
Cowton.

Description: A very attractive and fairly new fishery, Cornhill
offers three ponds. Pond 1 is the smallest at about half an
acre, it also has the smaller silver fish including perch and
gudgeon. The other two ponds are around one and a half
acres and have islands to target the good sized carp and
tench. Each has a four foot shelf around the edge, going to
around six foot in the centre.

Types of Fish: Stocked with many species including, carp to
27lbs, tench to around 7lbs, roach, perch and crucians.
Also rudd, gudgeon and plenty of bream. You will also find
blue and golden orfe present.

Rules/Bans: Barbless hooks only. No groundbait.

Facilities: **Number of Lakes:** Three

Sat Nav: DL7 0JW   **Telephone:** 01325 378662

Elvington Lake

Wheldrake Lane, Elvington, Nr York.

Ticket Price: 2 Rods £4.00, 3 or more Rods £5.00

Directions: Leave the A64 and take the A1079. After a short distance take a right turn onto the B1228 signposted for Elvington. Go past the Air Museum entrance and then take a right turn down Wheldrake Lane. The water is a couple of miles down on your right hand side.

Description: The water is very well maintained and monitored by the owner. You generally have to get there early if you want the peg that is fishing well. It is very popular with specimen carp anglers. As you can gather there are some big fish here, reaching the high twenties. The lake is about 3 acres in size and offers some good features and secluded corners where fish can be caught. Tench and bream run to around 9lbs. Maggot or caster will get bites throughout the day, but make sure you don't fish too light or you might get snapped by something rather large!

Types of Fish: There are plenty of large carp, tench, bream, perch, roach, chub, and a few rudd.

Facilities:

Rules/Bans: Barbless Hooks only. Groundbait via the pole cup or feeder only. Fishing only from 8.00 am to 9pm. No litter.

Number of Lakes: One   **Sat Nav:** YO41 4AZ

Telephone: 01904 608255

Gascoigne Wood Fishery

Sherburn in Elmet.

Ticket Price: Day ticket £5.00. £4.00 Concessions.

Directions: Come off the A1 junction signposted Selby. Turn left at the junction with the A162. After a couple of miles turn right into Common Lane. If you pass under the railway, you have missed it. Travel down Common Lane for around half a mile. Go over the first railway bridge and as you approach the second railway bridge, turn left and the road leads you straight to the fishery.

Description: The larger of the two ponds is close to the carpark and has good access to a couple of pegs for disabled anglers. The average depth is five feet, but in the middle it does drop to near eight. This pond is excellent all year round. Both ponds hold a good variety of fish, with the odd carp to 18lb. plus many in the low doubles.

Types of Fish: Bream, Ide to 1lb, a selection of carp to 18lb, crucian to 1lb. Plenty of tench to 4lb, roach to 1lb, Rudd, Perch and Chub .

Rules/Bans: No keepnets. Barbless hooks only. Groundbait in feeder only and all under 16s must be accompanied by an adult. Litter will not be tolerated on this fishery and a strict "take it home with you" policy is in operation !

Facilities: **Number of Lakes:** Two

Sat Nav: LS25 5DL   **Telephone:** 0796 0136870

 7

Grange Farm Lake
York Road, Thirsk.

Ticket Price: Day ticket £5.00   Under 16's £3.00 accompanied by an adult.

Directions: Take the A19 (York Road) from Thirsk and head towards York. Take a left turn after about a mile and drive along the lay-by until the end and you will see the lake.

Description: This very attractive lake is set within a small static caravan site. It has an average depth of around 6 feet, but in the middle it is nearer 11feet. There is a good head of bream, plus a few large carp upto 20lb. The good sized tench take sweetcorn all day long. If you fancy catching a bag load of crucians then try a single maggot or caster. The winter fishing here is great, with some pike to 16lb. present.

Types of Fish: Carp to 20lb, pike, crucian carp, chub to 5lb, perch, tench, bream to 7lb, and roach to nearly 2lb.

Rules/Bans: No Keepnets. No litter. Barbless hooks only.

Facilities: **Number of Lakes:** One

Sat Nav: YO7 3AD   **Telephone:** 01845 522247

8

Hoxne Farm Ponds
Sheriff Hutton Rd, Strensall.

Ticket Price: Adult £5 , £3 juniors, £4 OAP, £1 extra per rod.

Directions: From the A1237 York ring road, take the Strensall turning off the roundabout. Follow signs into the village, past the Half Moon pub on the left. Turn left after the Ship Inn towards Sheriff Hutton. The ponds are located 1/2 mile on the right hand side.

Description: The fishery consists of three very productive ponds covering a total of approx 3 acres. The ponds are landscaped and have rushes & lily pads. There are 80 pegs in total. The ponds fish well whatever the season. Large carp are mainly caught on pellets, sweetcorn and maggots. Meat and hemp also do well. Try fishing on the top in the summer.

Types of Fish: Carp to 30lbs, bream to 7lbs, tench to 7lbs, roach to 2lbs, rudd, chub etc.

Rules/Bans: Day tickets must be obtained before fishing. All landing nets must be dipped before fishing. Keepnets in matches only. All fish must be netted. All hooks will be checked. Barbless hooks only, maximum size 12. Minimum hook length 2lb. breaking strain. No floating baits, boilies, nuts, bloodworm or joker. No catmeat, method feeders, braid or dogs. Groundbait in pole cups or feeders only. No free-lining. No litter.

Facilities: **Number of Lakes:** Three

Telephone: 01904 490726   **Sat Nav:** YO32 5TL

Langwith Lakes
Langwith Lane, Heslington, York.

Ticket Price: £5.00 Adult. £4.00 Concessions. £4.00 Under 16's. One Rod Only.

Directions: Come off the A64 outer ring road and follow signs for University of York. At the first roundabout turn left to Heslington. At the next junction turn left into the village of Heslington. Go through the village until you come to a mini-roundabout, take a right turn and follow the lane for 2 miles to a 'T' junction. Turn right. Langwith Lakes is on the left.

Description: There are four newly constructed lakes at Langwith. Kevin's Lake with depths to 4 1/2 feet, stocked with thousands of match size carp (mirrors, common, ghost and F1 hybrids) to 5lb. Also roach, chub, skimmers and tench including hundreds of golden tench. Bethany's Lake with depths to 3 1/2 feet. Stocked as Kevin's Lake. Anya's Lake and Emma's Lake have depths to 4 1/2 feet. Both are stocked as Kevin's Lake but also have a good head of barbel.

Rules/Bans: Day tickets must be obtained before fishing.
All landing nets must be dipped before fishing. Keepnets in matches only. All fish must be netted. All hooks will be checked. Barbless hooks only, maximum size 12. Minimum hook length 2lb. breaking strain. No floating baits, boilies, nuts, bloodworm or joker. No catmeat, method feeders, braid or dogs. Groundbait in pole cups or feeders only. No free-lining. No litter.

Facilities: ♿ 🅿 🚻   **Number of Lakes:** Four
Sat Nav: YO10 5EJ

Telephone: 01904 431874 **Mob:** 07969 522402

Lingcroft Farm Pond
Fulford, York.

Ticket Price: Day ticket £5.00. Under 16's must be accompanied by an adult.

Directions: Take the A19 out of York and head south. Stay on the A19 till you've past the A64 junction. Then turn right towards Lingcroft Farm

Description: This pond is a former moat and has a cobbled yard on the island in the centre. Unfortunately it is not possible to get on to the island for a closer look. Fishing is restricted to nine anglers so come early, especially at weekends. Luncheon meat and corn work well for the carp which do seem to show all over this pond, but I would try fishing in the shaded area near the island. The large head of roach were taking pellet and worm and of course maggots.

Types of Fish: Carp to 18lbs. Roach that reach 1lb. There may also be a few other species.

Rules/Bans: Barbless hooks only. No keepnets.

Facilities:

Number of Lakes:
One

Sat Nav:
YO19 4RE

Telephone:
01904 629773

23

The Mere, Barlow Common
Selby.

Ticket Price: Day ticket £5.00 for 1 rod, 2nd rod £1.00
Season Permits: Adult £27. Concession £16. Family £33.

Directions: Barlow Common is easily reached from the A1041 Selby to Snaith Road by taking the southern-most turning to Barlow Village. The main entrance and carpark, which is free of charge, are located on the left 2/3 miles from the A1041.

Description: This four acre lake is set within the Barlow Common Local Nature Reserve. It has 25 well placed pegs and a depth of twelve feet at its deepest. Over the last few years the lake has been heavily stocked with around 900 tench and 100 bream. Feeder fishing for the tench worked well for a local young angler. He was using luncheon meat with a ground bait mix in his open ended feeder. He had lost count of the number of fish he had caught, but he wasn't going to forget the 7lb carp which was a surprise.

Types of Fish: Stocked with tench, bream, roach, rudd, perch and common / mirror carp.

Rules/Bans: No tins on the bank. No night fishing. No keepnets. Children under 14 must be accompanied by an adult.

Facilities:

Telephone: 01757 617110   **Number of Lakes:** One

24

Mushroom Ponds
Mill Lane, South Milford.

Ticket Price: Day ticket £5.00. OAP's £4.00. Under 16's must be accompanied by an adult.

Directions: From junction 42 of the A1(M) head east on the A63. Turn left onto the A162. On reaching South Milford, turn left opposite the Swan pub into High Street. Turn right into Mill Lane. Mushroom farm and fishery is at the end of the lane.

Description: Their are three ponds holding upto forty anglers at any one time. The Far Pool holds the larger carp but all three have the same species stocked. Float fish soft hookable pellets in the summer months and maggot and caster in the cooler conditions. There is a small island in the first pool you come too, try feeder fishing meat to either side for the many carp present. Depths between 7-10 feet.

Types of Fish: Bream and tench to 4lbs. large roach and rudd. Carp to 17lb. Some small barbel. Chub, ide, golden orfe and perch make up the remaining species.

Rules/Bans: Barbless hooks only.
No keepnets except for matches.

Facilities: 🅿 ♿ 🚻 🍴   Sat Nav: LS25 5AG

Number of Lakes: Three   **Telephone:** 01977 684693

The Oaks Lakes Fishery
Sessay, Nr Thirsk.

Ticket Price: Adult £7.00. Concessions and after 4pm £4.00.

Directions: Exit A1 at junction 49 onto the A168 heading to Thirsk. Come off at the next exit (sign posted Dalton). Turn Right off the slip road. Go underneath the flyover. Take next right (200 yds). Go through Dalton village. At the T junction turn right (Sessay). Go past the Moor & Pheasant pub, and over a railway bridge. The fishery is 400 yds on the left.

Description: There are 4 main match lakes at The Oaks; Cedar (matches only), Poplar, Maple and Alders. The other 3 lakes, Firs, Oaks and Willows are always open to allow pleasure fishing. Firs Lake is my favourite with a depth of 5 feet, plenty of reeds to target and surrounded by trees, which protect you from the wind.

Types of Fish: Tench, bream, carp, perch, roach, chub, ide, rudd, barbel, golden orfe, crucian and gudgeon.

Rules/Bans: No Keepnets after 4pm. Barbless hooks only.

Number of Lakes: Seven

Facilities:

Telephone: 01845 501321   **Sat Nav:** YO7 3BJ

Oaktree Leisure

Baston Lane, Huby.

Ticket Price: Day ticket £5.00. Concessions £3.00.

Directions: From York take the A19 York to Thirsk Road and turn right at Tollerton crossroads. Follow this road to Huby for about one and a half miles. The fishery is located on the right hand side of the road.

Description: This well maintained, fairly new, four lake complex is well worth a visit. All four lakes have Islands to target the larger carp which weigh around 20lb. A lot of the carp are single figure fish which makes this venue ideal for pole and waggler anglers. Tench and bream are also stocked along with good numbers of roach.

Types of Fish: Carp to 20lb. Tench, bream, roach and a small numbers of other species.

Rules/Bans: Barbless hooks only.
No hooks bigger than size 12. No method feeder.
No trout pellets. No keepnets.

Facilities: Cafe on Sundays. Toilets. Disabled parking near the ponds.

Number of Lakes: Four   **Sat Nav:** Not available

Telephone: 01347 810686

Paradise Lakeside

Ballhall Lane, Storwood, York.

Ticket Price: Day tickets £10. No concessions.

Directions: From York join the A1079 signposted for Hull. Turn immediate right onto the B1228 signposted for Elvington. Travel through Elvington and over the river Derwent. Travel through Sutton Upon Derwent and cross Pocklington canal at Hagg Bridge. Ignore the first turning for Storwood. After a couple of hairpin bends, turn right at the second signpost to Storwood. You will find the fishery approximately 500 metres on your left.

Description: There are two ponds here, but only Pond One is for day ticket fishing, the other is for residents only. It has twenty pegs and contains a wide variety of lilies and reed beds situated around two islands from which to stalk your quarry. The pond is set in a mature oak woodland.
It contains tench, rudd, roach, perch and crucian carp to 2.5lb. Bream to 3lb, plus mirror and common carp to 20lb+ and golden orfe to 2.5lb.

Rules/Bans: No keepnets. Barbless hooks only. No Radios. No pets. No litter. No fires. Groundbait in moderation. Under 16's must be accompanied by an adult.

Number of Lakes: One   **Sat Nav:** Y042 4TD

Facilities: accommodation in lodges available.

Telephone: 01759 318452   16

Parklands Fishery

Yafforth Road, Yafforth.

Ticket Price: Day ticket £6.00.   Concessions £5.00.

Directions: From Northallerton take the B6271 towards Yafforth (signposted from the town). After about a mile, just before you get to another turn off for Romanby, you will see a sign for the fishery on your right. Follow the track to the carpark.

Description: Parklands has two lakes, Kingfisher with 37 pegs and Parklands lake with 15 pegs. The depths vary from 3 foot to almost 7 foot in places. Both lakes are stocked with carp of all sizes, the largest being 20lbs. There is secure parking with toilet facilities. Some of the closer pegs are suitable for disabled anglers, but anglers using wheelchairs will be restricted. Fishing with pole or waggler works well, or try a method feeder for the carp.

Types of Fish: Stocked with most species of fish including, carp to 20lbs, tench to around 6lbs, roach to 2lbs, perch and crucians upto 2lbs, rudd, barbel, gudgeon and plenty of bream to 4lbs. You may catch the odd chub as well.

Rules/Bans: Under 14's must be accompanied by an adult. No ground bait other than in pole cup or feeder, Barbless hooks only. No bloodworm or joker.

Facilities: **Number of Lakes:** One

Sat Nav: DL7 0LQ   **Telephone:** 01609 779140   17

Pool Bridge Farm
Wheldrake Lane, Crockey Hill, York.

Ticket Price: Day tickets are to be purchased from the cafe.
Adult: £6 for 1 Rod or £8 for 2 Rods.
Concessions: £5 for 1 Rod or £6 for 2 Rods.

Directions: Leave the A64 at the A19 turnoff (signposted "Designer Outlet") and head towards Selby for about a mile. At the traffic lights turn left and head towards Wheldrake. Follow this road (Wheldrake Lane) for about a mile and the entrance to the farm is on the left just before the road passes over a bridge.

Description: Pool Bridge Farm, also known as Fletcher's, is a tranquil, picturesque fishery where you will find "The Q" Lake - a specimen carp fishing lake. The angling complex has a further four course fishing lakes which are well stocked with a large variety of silver fish including, Tench, Rudd, Roach, Bream and some very big Perch!

Rules/Bans: No Keepnets. Barbless hooks only. No Cat Meat. Groundbait may only be used in a small pole-cup or feeder. Please use all baits in moderation.
Under 16's must be accompanied by an adult.

Facilities: There is an on-site cafe as well as ladies, gents and disabled toilet facilities. Showers are also provided for those of you that are night fishing.

Number of Lakes: Five

Sat Nav: YO19 4SQ

Telephone: 01904 633340 or 07928 359420

Pottery Pond
Pottery Lane, Strensall.

Ticket Price: Day Tickets (6.30am until dusk) £5.00 for up to 2 rods, Extra rods £1.00 each, Senior Citizens £4.00. Under 16s (accompanied by an adult) £3.00. Evening Tickets (after 4.00pm) £4.00. Night Fishing (24 hours - by prior arrangement only) £15.00.

Directions: Approaching York, follow the outer ring road, A1237, until Strensall is signposted. Once in the main village street, at the Ship Inn take the Sheriff Hutton road over the bridge for about half a mile. Turn first left into Pottery Lane, signposted Sutton-on-the-Forest. A further half mile on your right is Pottery Pond.

Description: This venue is suited to the specimen angler or the angler looking for a challenge. This 54 peg lake is heavily stocked with Common and Mirror Carp, Crucian Carp, Pike, Roach, Rudd, Chub, Bream, Barbel, Perch, Tench and Gudgeon. Specimen fish caught this year include Pike to 31.5lb, Carp to 21.5lb, Tench to 10lb, Bream to 10lb, Crucian Carp to 3.5lb.

Rules/Bans: Barbless hooks only. Fish over 2lb not to be retained in keep nets. To avoid injury to wildlife, all loose line to be disposed of in a proper manner. Anglers must use only 1 peg at a time. No cars or trailers on the bank. No open fires or barbecues. No dogs except guide-dogs. All litter and cigarette ends to be removed by angler. Night fishing with prior permission.

Number of Lakes: One

Sat Nav: YO32 5TW

Facilities:

Telephone: 01347 810617

 19

Prospect Farm Pond
Penny Pot Lane, Harrogate.

Ticket Price: Day tickets £5.00. Under 16's: £3.00.
Tickets are bought from the farmhouse on the way in.

Directions: Take the A59 from Harrogate. Turn left onto the B6161. Take your next right into Penny Pot Lane. The fishery is down the farm lane on your left.

Description: This natural 0.6 acre pond is set in a very attractive location, which is bordered to one side by a wood. It has been extensively stocked with a variety of species. Both tench and carp show to float fished corn. Leger meat to the centre of the pond for the larger carp. Average depths are only four feet so don't fish with too heavier weights. The carp congregate very close to the small island, especially in the warmer months.

Types of Fish: Tench, bream to 4lb. Rudd, roach, perch, and carp to 18lb. Plus a few orfe.

Rules/Bans: No keepnets. Barbless hooks only. Night fishing by strict prior arrangement.

Facilities: Food outlet nearby. Toilets. Disabled access.

Number of Lakes: One   **Sat Nav:** HG3 1SQ

Telephone: 01423 507870

Queen Mary's Ponds
Black Heath Lake & Figure 8 Lake, Ripon.

Ticket Price: Membership permits and prices, see page 58.

Directions: From the A1 take the A61 to Ripon. At the clock tower turn right onto the A6108 signposted West Tanfield and continue for 1 mile. Turn right into the Ripon Golf and Tennis Club (Park Lane) and follow the lane, park next to signs at the end.

Description: Black Heath Lake is a four acre natural lake where each peg has a feature. Some of the largest carp in the club can be found in this water, feeding off the plentiful supplies of bloodworm beds. A beautiful water, away from general traffic, but easily accessible by car with average walks to pegs. Bream and tench are the heaviest stocked fish. In 2004 over 1,100 tench were stocked. 2002 saw Roach and Rudd stocked.

Figure 8 Lake is similar to Black Heath Lake, the banks of the two lakes are merely meters apart. Tackle needs to be heavy due to the specimen carp and tench, plus there are numerous snags. Each peg again has a feature and careful plumbing to find drops and shelves returns dividends of 100lb. pleasure bags.

Facilities: ♿ P

Sat Nav: HG4 3HJ

Telephone: Bradford No1 Angling Association

Rules/Bans: Permit Water Conditions.
1. Not more than 3 dates to be applied for at any one time.
2. Applications to be made with the Assistant Secretary 7 days before required date.
3. Members must not apply for permits until the last date on their permit expires.

This water is very heavily bailiffed. Fishing without a permit on this water will lead to an immediate ban.

Information kindly supplied by Bradford No1 Angling Association.

Raker Lakes

Greengales Lane, Wheldrake, York.

Ticket Price: Day tickets (Course) £6.00 adult. £4.00 Conc.
Kingfisher Lake (Carp) £10 per day (upto 3 rods).

Directions:

Description:
Raker Lakes consists of 4 coarse lakes and a specimen
lake, catering for match, pleasure and specimen anglers.
There is also a small touring caravan site. Set in 28 acres of
beautiful countryside, this venue is well worth a visit. Try
Highbank Lake for a mixed bag of silver fish along with
some good sized carp.

Types of Fish: Tench, bream, rudd, roach, crucian, chub,
perch, and many species of large carp.

Rules/Bans: All landing nets must be dipped. Barbless
hooks only. No keepnets. Groundbait in feeders or pole
cups only (not by hand). No nuts, bloodworm or joker.
Poles may be floated on water providing a float is attached.
No children unless fishing - children under 14 must be
accompanied by an adult. No dogs, radios or fires.
Check for additional rules applying to Kingfisher Lake.

Number of Lakes: Five   **Sat Nav:** Y019 6BW

Facilities:

22

Telephone: 01904 448793

Raskelf Lake
West Moor Road, Raskelf.

Ticket Price: Membership permits and prices, see page 58.

Directions: Travel through Boroughbridge and over the River. At the next roundabout take the 3rd exit. Continue on this road and take the 1st Right. Follow the road until Thornton Bridge, take a right and cross over the river and keep going through Milby and straight on to the Junction opposite the Oak Tree pub. Turn left and travel over a small hump backed bridge. Go over the next hump and straight after turn right and enter fishery.

Description: A well established lake in a former brick pit. The depth is an even 5 feet in most places. The locals have several names for various parts of the lake. To the left of entry is the orchard area. Here there are several well established weed beds and the water is shallower than average. This is home to the many tench to 6lb.+ and several big carp to 27lb. To the right at the far end is the area known as the Railway End. Here there is a rod length and pole limit in place of 13 feet. This is the place to catch large nets of smaller roach, rudd, tench and bream plus the occasional carp. The far side of the lake is called the Field Side and again is shallower. This is home to larger tench and carp, plus some of the older bream. Raskelf is one of the only waters where a match can be won from any peg, and a water which responds to little and often feeding. Being near to the river it also gets more than its fair share of eels, and some monster specimens to 5lb have been recorded.

Number of Lakes: One

Information kindly supplied by Bradford No1 Angling Association.

Telephone: Bradford No1 Angling Association

Facilities:

Rawcliffe Lake

Oakdale Road, Rawcliffe, York.

Ticket Price: £5.00 per day in advance only from York tackle shops.

Directions: From York take the A19 Thirsk road. When you reach Rawcliffe, turn right onto the A1237 ring road. Turn right into Clifton Moorgate and right again onto Oakdale Road. You wil find the carpark on your right.

Description: This council owned 5 acre lake is run by York and District Amalgamation of Anglers. One of the best waters, so close to the centre of York. At only 4 feet deep it is ideal for the novice angler with plenty of quality fish to target. Try luncheon meat or sweet corn using an open feeder for the carp that reach 20lb. Soft hookable pellets work well for the bream, red maggot for the roach and perch.

Types of Fish: Carp to 20lb, bream to over 6lb, plenty of tench to 3lb. Other species present are roach, perch and crucian carp.

Rules/Bans: Dawn till dusk only. Barbless hooks only, no keepnets.

Number of Lakes: One   **Telephone:** 01904 651346

Facilities: **Sat Nav:** YO30 4YL

Red House Lagoon
Moor Monkton.

Ticket Price: £5.00 per day in advance only from York tackle shops.

Directions: From York you need to take the A59, to Knaresborough. You pass through Nether and Upper Poppleton. Turn right (signposted) to Moor Monkton. You then need to take the first right, which will lead you down to the water.

Description: Another water controlled by York and District Amalgamation of Anglers. This very exposed crescent shaped lake has 40 pegs and plenty of features to target. You can fish close in as the water is around 8 feet at only a rods distance. Fishing red maggot with a bit of hemp will keep the roach and perch in your swim all day. Target the bream using a feeder with worm or sweet corn on the hook.

Types of Fish: Roach, perch, bream, there are quite a number of large pike to catch during the winter months.

Number of Lakes: One

Rules/Bans: You can fish from dawn until dusk.
No groundbait or livebaiting allowed. Barbless hooks only.

Facilities:

Sat Nav: Not Available

Telephone: 01904 651346

Redwood Park
Tollerton Rd, Huby, York.

Ticket Price: Daily rate is £5.00 Concessions £4.00 (£4.00 if you arrive after 4pm).

Directions: Head out of York on the A19. Stay on this road for about 10 miles, going through Skelton and Skipton. At Cross Lanes turn right and you will find the fishery about half a mile on your right.

Description: This fishery was brand new in 2008. It has two lakes both stocked with a variety of fish which range between 3lb and 5lb. Arc Lake is 25m wide, which is ideal for those wanting to use a waggler or feeder approach. Depths are very even along the length of the lake, so it isn't too 'peggy'. Redwood Lake has 32 pegs spaced out along its banks. The lake depth variations from 4.5ft to 11ft, with an island to one end.

Types of Fish: Stocked with roach, bream, tench, carp, crucian carp, chub, and rudd.

Rules/Bans: No Keepnets. Barbless hooks only. No floating poles. Fishing from numbered pegs only. All landing nets must be dipped. Only one rod to be used at any time. Groundbait can be used in moderation. All fish of 4 ounce or greater must be netted. No litter to be left on site. No fish to be removed from site. No boilies. No bivvies. No electronic bite alarms.

Facilities: ♿ P 🚹 🍽   **Number of Lakes:** Two

Sat Nav: YO61 1JE   **Telephone:** 07909 956532   26

Rolieth Fishery

Otterington Park, South Otterington, Northallerton.

Ticket Price: £5 for adults, £3 for juniors under 14 and OAPs.

Directions: See Map.

Description: This small acre pond is well stocked with a variety of silver fish. Its situated within a caravan site where you could stay in static caravans or cabin style lodges. The lake has plenty of reed beds to target and good well spaced out pegs. This pond holds a massive head of perch as well as roach to a 1lb and some quality tench to 4lbs.

Types of Fish: Bream, roach, perch, rudd, tench and Crucian Carp.

Rules/Bans: Barbless hooks only.
No keepnets.

Number of Lakes: One

Facilities:

Sat Nav: DL7 9JB   **Telephone:** 01609 780656   27

39

Rosedale Fishery
Bridlington Road, Hunmanby.

Ticket Price: Daily rate is £5.00 Concessions £4.00

Directions: Rosedale Fishery can be found on the outskirts of Hunmanby on the Bridlington Road. Head south to Driffield, go over the level crossing and you will see a signpost for the fishery.

Description: This well established lake is about six acres in size. Each of the 42 pegs are nicely secluded and surrounded by trees. It has a well deserved reputation for being a productive all year round fishery.
Catches of over 100lb are possible especially as there are so many good sized carp present, with some specimens running to 27lbs. Try peg 7 on the south bank where you can catch plenty of bream on corn or soft hookable pellets.

Types of Fish: Stocked with carp which average 5-7lb plus some to 27lb. Roach, bream, tench and skimmers.

Rules/Bans: No Keepnets except in matches. Barbless hooks only. No floating baits, Hook lengths must be used at all times. No fixed rig method fishing. Dogs must be on a lead at all times. Juniors must be accompanied by an adult. No hooks over a size 10.

Facilities: **Number of Lakes:** One

Sat Nav: YO14 0LR   **Telephone:** 07717 666921

Scalm Park Ponds
Wistow, Selby.

Ticket Price: Carp Pond/Horse Shoe £5 for one rod £7.50 for two. Mixed Pond £4 for one £6 for two.
Open from dawn to dusk.

Directions: →

Description: The Mixed Pond is my favourite of the three ponds available to fish at Scalm. The water has depths between 4 and 8 ft. There is a mixture of fish in here with plenty of reeds and marginal features to target. Traditional baits will see you catching tench, rudd and bream whilst the bigger baits tend to find the carp. Margin fishing with a short pole will get you plenty of bites, but pick your peg well as some are a lot more productive than others. Feeder fishing further out is worth a try for the larger carp. The Carp Lake is set in the middle of the golf course and is long and thin. Watch out for the stray golf ball.

Types of Fish: Carp in excess of 20lbs, tench, rudd, bream and chub.

Rules/Bans: Barbless hooks only. No boilies or fires. No fish 3lb plus to be kept in keepnets. 2lb minimum line on the carp pond.

Facilities: P ♿ 🚻 🍔 🚐

Sat Nav: YO8 3RD

Number of Lakes: Three   **Telephone:** 01757 210846

 29

Scarborough Mere
Mere Lane, Scarborough.

Ticket Price: Specimen Lake £5.00 one rod, £8.00 for two. Match Lake and Ski Pool £5.00 one rod only. Day tickets available on the bank. This venue is run by the Scarborough Mere Angling Club.

Directions: Take the A64 Seamer Road from Scarborough. The water is on your left just below Oliver's Mount.

Description: The Mere is split into three parts. The largest 9-acre Specimen Pool has carp upto 30lbs., tench which reach 10lb. and some heavy bream at 14lbs. Carp to 15lb., bream, tench, perch, roach and crucians can be found in the 2-acre Match Lake. Ski Pool has large pike to nearly 28lbs., smaller carp to 7lb and a mixture of silver fish. Groundbait feeder works well for the bream using either maggot or caster as your hook bait. Fish to the islands on the Specimen Lake for the large carp.

Rules/Bans: No keepnets on the Match Lake.
Barbless hooks only.

Facilities:

Number of Lakes: Three **Sat Nav:** YO11 2YN

Telephone: 01723 507588

Selby 3 Lakes

Bawtry Road, Selby.

Ticket Price: First 24 hours: £20. Per 24 hours after: £15.
All swims must be prebooked beforehand by calling Gordon
Fowler on 07818 092420.

Directions: Enter Selby on Bawtry Road A1041. Pass the
cattle market on your left hand side and you will
immediately see the new housing estate on the right. Take a
left turn signposted Selby Three Lakes Industrial Estate.
The lake is situated along the right hand side of this road.
Parking is located immediately on the right in the car park
with the sandwich van.

Description: Many years ago there were 3 lakes here, hence
the name, but Selby 3 Lakes is a one carp lake fishery.
There has been extensive restocking over the past year, with
some very big fish. The Lake is available for carp fishing
only with a maximum of 10 Anglers, and all 10 places must
be Pre-Booked.

Types of Fish: Carp

Rules/Bans: 3 Rods maximum. No Keepnets. No dogs
No litter. No carp sacks. No bent hooks. No Long-Shank
Nailers. No line under 12lb to a baited rod. No leadcore.
No shock leaders. No remote controlled boats or dinghies.
No particles (beans, seeds or nuts). No trout pellets.
No fixed leads. Large unhooking mats must be used.

Facilities: **Number of Lakes:** One

Sat Nav: YO8 8NB   **Telephone:** 07818 092420

43

Southfield Fisheries

Southfield Farm, Rainton Lane, Dishforth.

Ticket Price: Adults £6.00. Juniors / OAP £5.00.

Directions: Situated between Rainton and Dishworth Villages on the Rainton side of the Dishforth Interchange. From the South, leave the A1 at Boroughbridge and head north towards Dishforth on the A168.

Description: The 2 ponds at Southfield are spring fed which greatly enhances the quality of the water and the fish. Disabled anglers can park cars by some pegs and close to others. Pegs on the bottom pond have guard rails. There is a toilet available with disabled facilities. The fishery is open all year round unless the ponds have frozen. Match bookings can be arranged.

Types of Fish: Pond A : Mixed coarse including Roach, Rudd, Crucians, Bream, and Carp to 8lb.
Pond B : Carp to 22lb, Tench and Roach to 1 1/2lb.

Rules/Bans: EA Rod licence is required. Barbless hooks only. Keepnets in matches only. Anglers must be in possession of an assembled landing net. Carp landing mats to be used for any fish over 8lb. Groundbait in feeders only. Nets must be dipped in tanks provided by pond A. Juniors under 14 years must be accompanied by an adult.

Facilities: **Number of Lakes:** Two

Sat Nav: YO7 3DA   32

Telephone: 01765 640231

44

Stonebridge Fishing Lakes
Fleetham Lane, Scruton, Northallerton.

Ticket Price: Coarse (St Claudes Lake) £6.00
Carp Lake £8.00. Trout Lake also available.

Directions: located close to the village of Scruton near Northallerton in North Yorkshire. The quickest route is to use either the A684 or the A1 trunk road.

Description: St. Claudes Lake covers approximately 7 acres and contains both carp and silvers. This lake has been newly stocked and has 46 pegs. The Carp Lake is approximately 4 Acres. This lake is in a natural bulrush environment and has 10 pegs available at any one time. The lake has only recently been re-opened to the angler. Recent reports show that there are many fish that are 'virgin' (Never been caught before) in this lake.

Rules/Bans: Barbless hooks only (no micro barbs). No fish above 5lbs to be held in keep nets. No trout pellets or high oil pellets. Maximum hooksize 12. Only 1kg. of ground bait to be used per visit. No fixed ledger methods allowed. Running leads only. No floating bait. No cat meat (luncheon meat only). No Braid. Only Stonebridge nets to be used. Fishing from designated pegs only. All litter to be taken away. Keepnets must not be used by leisure anglers.

Number of Lakes: Two coarse, one trout.

Facilities: ♿ 🅿 🚻
Food available to order.

Sat Nav: DL7 0RR
Telephone: 01609 748818

33

45

Sunrise Lakes

Haggs Road, Spofforth.

Ticket Price: Day tickets £6.00. Extra rod £3.00. Evening summer tickets £4.00 after 4pm. Concessions £5.00. Pay on your way in, not on the bank.

Directions: Take the A661 from Wetherby, heading towards Spofforth. Go through Spofforth, over the roundabout and turn left into Haggs Road. Turn left between two telegraph poles, signposted to the fishery. Follow this track to the car park.

Description: This attractive well maintained mixed fishery has three lakes. North Lake has 25 pegs, with carp to 14lbs and many more species including barbel and chub. South Lake has the bigger carp and similar stocks as North Lake.
The Match lake has 60 pegs and is packed again with most species. The depths varies between 4 and 7 feet. Take your pick on baits but don't forget maggots in the winter months.

Rules/Bans: No keepnets. Barbless hooks only. Other rules posted.

Facilities:

Number of Lakes: Three   **Sat Nav:** Not available.

Telephone: 07979 803207

Thorpe Underwood Lake
Thorpe Underwood.

Ticket Price: Membership permits and prices, see page 58.

Directions: →

Description: A purpose dug club lake of around 6 acres at the edge of the River Ouse, in pleasant quite surroundings behind the local nursing college. This water is stream fed and feeds into the River Ouse. There are two lakes on the site, the club lake is the one nearest the river. Depths vary from around 18" to 10 feet in the middle of the lake. No fishing is allowed on the lake on the left. The main species in the lake are the many recently stocked bream and skimmers which run to around 3lb. There are also tench and chub which have grown to around the 4lb mark. There is also a very large head of roach and rudd. Eels and pike are present which have made their way into the lake during recent floods. Some specimen perch can also be found around the weedier swims. Groundbait or maggot feeder fished towards the middle can account for some fine nets of fish. Pole or waggler fished in areas from 3 to 4 feet can see good tench and roach. Generally on this water, when the bream are caught it indicates a good days sport is on the cards. Little and often is the best approach for the silver fish, and a sit it out approach is best for the bream.

Facilities:

Rules/Bans: No keepnets. Barbless hooks only.

Telephone: Bradford No1 Angling Association

Sat Nav: YO26 9SJ

Information kindly supplied by Bradford No1 Angling Association.

Tollerton Ponds
Cross lane Ends, Tollerton.

Ticket Price: Day tickets are £6.00. Concessions £4.00.

Directions: Head north from York on the A19. Go through Shipton. Don't take the first Tollerton turning, carry on for about one mile on the A19. Then turn left into the fishery.

Description: Three ponds to chose from. Heron Lake has 20 pegs and three islands to target the carp that reach 10lbs. Most species of silver fish are also present in this lake. Kingfisher also has 20 pegs and is slightly deeper than the other lakes at 6 feet in the middle. Coot Lake is the smallest with 18 pegs, but does hold the larger carp up to 15lbs along with eels to 5lb. Most people were pole fishing, soft pellet or corn and were catching a mixed bag.

Types of Fish: Tench, bream, carp, roach, rudd, crucian carp, chub, ide and eel.

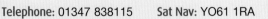

Rules/Bans: Barbless hooks only. All fish to be landed with a net. No cloths to be used when handling fish. No catfood allowed or floating baits.

Number of Lakes: Three

Facilities:

Telephone: 01347 838115   **Sat Nav:** YO61 1RA

36

Weeton Pond
Wayside Terrace, Huby.

Ticket Price: Adults £6.00. Concessions £5.00.
Tickets from the house on the way in or on the bank.

Directions: Head towards Harrogate on the A658. When you reach Huby turn right into Wayside Terrace. The pond is set in the grounds of the last house on your right, before the railway bridge.

Description: This one acre pond is in the owner's back garden and is perfect for both pole or waggler fishing. There is a central island and plenty of reed beds to target the plentiful carp that reach an impressive 23lb. Pellet, meat or corn for the carp, maggot or worm for the bream and ide. This is a nice safe shallow pond at around 4ft. Perfect for the disabled and the novice angler.

Types of Fish: Carp, bream, ide and roach.

Rules/Bans: Barbless hooks only.
Fishing from 8am until dusk. Keepnet restrictions apply.

Number of Lakes: One

Facilities: Toilets and showers are available. Disabled access. Food outlet nearby. Log cabin accommodation planned for the future.

Telephone: 07793 200822 or 01423 734062

Sat Nav: LS17 0HE

Whitehouse Farm Lakes
Thirsk Road, Easingwold.

Ticket Price: £5.00 on the bank. No concessions.

Directions: Head towards York on the A19. Go through Thormandy. Continue on the A19 until you reach a roundabout. Take the Thirsk Road, signposted Easingwold. You will find the fishery at the second farm entrance on your right. It is only 500 yards from the roundabout.

Description: Anglers favour the corners pegs at this privately owned three lake fishery. It is ideal for families offering fishing for all abilities. Stackyard Pond has only six well spaced pegs and contains carp to 10lbs. In the warmer months try fishing large chunks of luncheon meat or multiple pieces of sweetcorn. Soft hookable pellet seemed to attract all species when fished on a short pole close to the reeds.

Types of Fish: Ghost carp to 19lb. Tench to 4lbs. Some good sized rudd, roach and crucian carp to nearly 2lbs. Chub and perch make up the remaining species.

Rules/Bans: Under 16's must be accompanied by an adult. No carp over 5lbs. in keepnets. Barbless hooks only.

Facilities: Food outlet nearby.

Number of Lakes: Three

38

Telephone: 07974 090323   **Sat Nav:** YO61 3NF

The Willows

A59, Hessay, York.

Ticket Price: Adults £6.00 Concessions £5.00.
After 4pm £4.00.

Directions: From York head west on the A59. The fishery is on your right hand side just before you reach Hessay.

Description: This fishery boasts many feature-rich pegs, offering great coarse and carp fishing for the pleasure, or match angler. The Ridge Pool is the smaller of the two ponds at just over an acre. It has 26 pegs and many features including water lillies and overhanging willow trees. Goldrush is around 3 acres and is heavily stocked with many species including golden tench to 3lb.

Types of Fish: Carp to 10lb, crucian carp to 2lb, tench to 5lb, golden tench to 3lb, roach to 2lb, chub to 3lb, ide to 3lb, rudd to 2lb, barbel to 3lb, grass carp to 5lb, Bream to 4lb.

Rules/Bans: Barbless hooks only, No keepnets - only one rod to be used at any one time. No night fishing. Please keep to the permanent pegs. Mini pellets only - No nuts, boilies, dead / live baiting, method feeders or braid hook lengths. No litter, discarded fishing tackle or bait. No pets allowed. Children under 14 must be accompanied by an adult.

Facilities: **Number of Lakes:** Two 39

B & B
available.   **Sat Nav:** Y026 8JU   **Telephone:** 01904 738206

51

Woodland Lakes

Carlton Miniot, Thirsk.

Ticket Price: Adults £8.00. Concessions £7.00. Juniors £6.00.

Directions: From Thirsk take the A61 (Carlton Road). Go through Carlton Miniot. Turn left as the road bends right. Follow the lane down to the fishery.

Description: This picturesque fishery is located in the heart of North Yorkshire, situated between the Hambleton Hills and the Yorkshire Dales. With 350 pegs on this 13 lake site, you will always find a good spot even on bank holidays. Try the Dragon Fly Lake, fishing with luncheon meat or pellet. I also put a feeder out next to the island with red maggots and caught several carp between two and four pounds.

Types of Fish: Carp, Bream, Tench, Chub, Barbel, Rudd, Orfe, Roach.

Rules/Bans: No keepnets. Barbless hooks only. No Radios. No litter.

Number of Lakes: Five pleasure lakes. Eight match lakes.

Facilities: Sat Nav: Y07 4NJ

accommodation in   Tackle shop also on site. lodges available.

Telephone: 01845 527099 or 07831 824870

52

Wykeham Lakes

Long Causeway Rd, Nr Scarborough.

Ticket Price: Coarse Lakes £7.00. (2 rods) Concessions £5.00.

Directions: Wykeham Lakes fishing complex is situated half a mile off the A170 between Wykeham village and West Ayton within the Dawnay Estates.

Description: There are three coarse lakes and two trout lakes. Carp Lake is the one to fish. At approximately two acres it has 28 pegs with an average depth of 8 feet. This lake is perfect for the angler who seeks an action packed day with fish coming thick and fast. This lake allows several different methods to be employed such as float, feeder and pole fishing.

Types of Fish: Carp, Tench, Crucian's, Roach, Perch, Chub, Bream, Rudd, and Pike.

Rules/Bans: Barbless/Micro-barbed hooks only are to be used (Semi Barbless trebles are acceptable for Pike fishing). Keepnets may be used on the Match Lake only. Unhooking mats are recommended for Pike and Carp over 5lb. Coarse Pellets only to be used. Non edible baits are not allowed i.e. artificial sweetcorn/ meat/bread etc.
No fixed leads/feeders are to be used. No dogs or radios.

Number of Lakes: Three Coarse, Two Trout.

Facilities:

Telephone: 07946 534001

Sat Nav: YO13 9QU

41

Keep a record of all your fishing trips with

Log-it

Venue:		Address:			Date:
Peg No:	Start Time:		End Time:	Weather Conditions:	

Species	Weight	Method	Rig set up	Ground Bait	Hook Bait	Time

Venue:		Address:			Date:
Peg No:	Start Time:		End Time:	Weather Conditions:	

Species	Weight	Method	Rig set up	Ground Bait	Hook Bait	Time

Venue:			Address:			Date:	
Peg No:	Start Time:		End Time:		Weather Conditions:		

Species	Weight	Method	Rig set up	Ground Bait	Hook Bait	Time

Bradford No1 Angling Association
Membership Fees & Agents

Subscriptions:

Juniors	(under 17 years old)	£14
Ladies		£16
Veteran	(over 65 years old)	£16
Full "Senior (male)"	(over 17 years old)	£36
Joining Fee	(not Juniors)	£20
Second rod permit	(allows 2nd rod on all venues)	£14
Privilege tickets	(allows a guest with full adult)	£3
Night Fishing	(Allows night fishing on either Knotford or Kirkless lagoons)	£50

Membership Permits are available from the following shops:

A.J.Jewsons Ltd
28 Horton Street
Halifax
tel: 01422 354146

Angling and Country Sports.
36 Cross green
Pool Road.
Otley
tel: 01943 462770

Chris Roberts Tackle
22 Chapel Hill
Huddersfield
tel: 01484 545032

Castleford Angling Supplies
143 Lower Oxford St
Castleford
tel: 01977 550465

Eccleshill Angling
13 Stoney Lane
Eccleshill
Bradford
tel: 01274 627989

Gee Tee
19A Briggate,
Silsden,
tel: 01535 - 655555

Grahams Fishing Tackle
87 Crossbank Rd
Batley
tel: 01924 442040

K.L. Tackle
127 North Street
Keighley
tel: 01535 667574

Kirkgate Anglers
95 Kirkgate
Leeds
tel: 0113 234 4880
www.tackle2u.com

Leeds Angling Centre
14 Branch Road.
Armley
tel: 0113 263 9333

Nigel Hirst
727Huddersfield Road
Ravensthorpe
Dewsbury
tel: 01924 491275

Outwood Angling
557-559 Leeds Road
Outwood
Wakefield
tel: 01924 835443

Tackle2U.com
905 Manchester Road
Bradford
tel: 01274 729570

Wibsey Angling
208 High Street
Wibsey
Bradford
tel: 01274 604542

Ring before visiting these shops for your permits, some may have stopped selling them.

FISHING TERMS

Here is a list of the words most commonly used. This will help anglers new to the sport to understand fishing terms used by other anglers.

BALE ARM: A revolving arm on a fixed spool reel which winds line onto the spool.

BAGGING UP: A term used when an angler is catching really well, or to describe a venue that is fishing well.

BAIT BANDS: These are small rubber bands. They are aimed at securing difficult to hook baits to the hook. They come in various sizes to accommodate the size of the bait.

BAITING NEEDLE: These pull the hair loop through the bait. They have a mechanism for attaching to the loop whether it is like a small hook, or a pivot that hooks over the loop. The needle is then drawn back through the bait taking the loop and hair with it.

BARBLESS: A type of hook without sharp barbs to help retain bait and fish. Barbed hooks are banned from most fisheries.

BIN LIDS: A slang term for large bream.

BITE ALARMS: These are electronic sensors that detect the movement of line caused by the fish. They usually have an audible alarm or light to alert the angler.

BIVIES: These are domed tents with an opening at the front providing a shelter from the elements.

BOILIES: These are generally hard balls of bait that are primarily designed as a carp bait.

BREAD PUNCH: A bread punch has a circular 'punch' at the end which is pushed down onto a slice of bread and cuts a small piece out which is placed on the hook. There are many different sizes of punches for different hook sizes.

BREAKING STRAIN: The amount of pressure a line will take before snapping.

BUMPED OFF: This term is used by pole anglers, whereby through the use of heavy tactics the fish once hooked is bumped off. This happens when the fish is not big enough to expand the elastic fully.

CASTERS: The chrysalis form of a maggot.

DEADBAITING: The use of dead fish for catching predatory fish such pike, perch, and eels.

DISGORGER: A long device to help remove the hook from a fish's mouth. Always have one with you.

FOUL HOOKED: A fish that has been hooked anywhere else on the body apart from the mouth.

GROUNDBAIT: A dry mixture intended to be thrown into the water to attract fish. Usually consists of bread crumb, crushed biscuit, crushed hemp or other ingredients.

HAIR RIG: A hair rig is generally a piece of line that extends beyond the point of the shank of the hook. On the end of the length of line is a small loop.

HOOKLENGTH: A short length of line, of lesser breaking strength than the mainline, to which the hook is tied. It is used to make it less likely to be detected by the fish. It also ensures that if the line is snapped by a fish, the angler would not then lose the float / swim feeder / leger and all the other shot

Legering: Bait held on the bottom by means of a weight or feeder.

Loosefeed: Small offerings of loose bait, such as maggots or sweetcorn, which are thrown into the water to keep the fish interested in the area you are fishing.

Line bites: False indications of bites usually caused by fish brushing against the line.

Lures: Artificial fish, used to tempt predators such as pike and zander.

Margin: This is an area nearest the bank, that has a shallower depth than that of the main water.

Match fishing: A competitive form of coarse fishing which involves people drawing out a random peg (a place to fish), and then trying to catch as many fish as possible within the allotted time. Usually the winner will be the one with the greatest weight of fish caught.

Peg: A peg is a pre defined fishing area. Venues are split up into evenly spaced fishing zones which are often marked with a wooden peg or marker.

Pinkies: The larvae of the green bottle fly. Small, very lively and great as a loosefeed on stillwaters and canals or as a hookbait for smaller fish.

Plummet: A device used for determining the depth of the water in which you are fishing.

Pole: A pole is constructed from very advanced carbon combinations and comes in various sizes, weight and prices.

Pole rig: These are lengths of line that have the float, weights and a hook attached.

Quiver tip: A special type of rod used to detect bites when ledgering. It has a sensitive tip that curves over when the angler has a bite. Quiver tips vary in strength and stiffness which can be changed according to the weather conditions.

Snags: Features in your swim that are likely to cause you problems They can also be fish holding features such as lilies, overhanging trees, sunken branches. A place to avoid once a fish is hooked.

Spade end hooks: Spade end hooks have an up-turned flattened piece of metal instead of an eye to which to tie the fishing line.

Specimen: A term given to any fish that is a particularly good size for its species.

Strike: To respond to the taking of the bait by pulling the rod in an upwards or sideways motion to hook the fish.

Swim: The area of water where you are fishing.

Tackle: A term used to refer to any fishing equipment (photo tackle)

Test curve: The test curve is the time and weight needed to make the tip bend 90 degrees from the rod butt. Each rod has a test curve with those being used for specimen fish such as carp having a greater test curve than a general coarse rod.

Trotting: Allowing a float to travel at the speed of the current.

Whip: This is a scaled down version of a pole.

North Yorkshire Tackle Shops

Acomb. 227 Hamilton Drive West, Acomb, York. YO24 4PL	01904 785237
Anglers Corner. 41 Huby Court, Walmgate, York. YO1 9UD	01904 629773
Baitbox Supplies. New House, Bagby, Thirsk. YO7 2PH	0870 1995590
Brown Trout. 26 Cold Bath Rd, Harrogate. HG2 0NA	01423 709741
Castle Foot Tackle. 1 Pier Terrace, Quay St, Scar, YO11 1PL	01723 370390
Elliott Angling. 87d Market Place, Thirsk. YO7 1ET	01845 574550
England Angling. Audax Close, Clifton Moor, York. YO30 4RA	01904 476476
Field Sports. 24-26, New St, Selby. YO8 4PT	01757 709607
Fish-n-Things. 5 Horsefair, Boroughbridge, York. YO51 9LF	01423 324776
G B Angling. 119 Victoria Rd, Scarborough. YO11 1SP	01723 365000
Gilsan Sports. 2 High St, Leyburn. DL8 5AQ	01969 623942
Gilsan Sports. 5 Market Place, Richmond. DL10 4HU	01748 822108
Harrogate Angling Supplies. 61 High St, Harrogate. HG2 7LQ	01423 883270
Hooks & Tackle. 40 Huntington Rd, York. YO31 8RE	01904 610357
Jackson's Fishing Tackle. 27 Albion Street, Earby. BB18 6QA	01282 843333
Linsley Brothers. 55 Tower St, Harrogate. HG1 1HS	01423 505677
Mitre Pets & Angling Centre. 212 Shipton Rd, York. YO30 5RZ	01904 654841
Northallerton Angling Centre. 4a Zetland St, Northallerton. DL6 1NA	01609 779140
Orvis. 1-22 West Park, Harrogate. HG1 1BJ	01423 561354
Phoenix Angling. Racecourse Rd, Scarborough. YO13 9HT	01723 865035
Reel Deal Tackle. 3 Bridge Rd, Richmond. DL10 7HB	01748 812828
Red Worms. Helperthorpe, Malton. YO17 8TQ	01944 738422
Richmond Angling centre. 8 Temple Square, Richmond. DL10 4EB	01748 822989
Ripon Angling Centre. 58-59 North Street, Ripon. HG4 1EN	01765 604666
Rods & Reels. 67, Church St, Whitby. YO22 4AS	01947 825079
Scarborough Angling. 7 Market Way, Scarborough. YO11 1HR	01723 381111
Selby Angling Centre. 69 Brook St, Selby. YO8 4AL	01757 703471
Swifts Tackle. 25 Castlegate, Malton. YO17 7DP	01653 694580
The Oaks Fishing Tackle Shop. Sessay, Thirsk. YO7 3BJ	01845 501003
Whitby Angling Supplies. 65, Haggersgate, Whitby. YO21 3PP	01947 603855
Woodland Tackle Shop. Carlton Miniott, Thirsk. YO7 4NJ	01845 526110
www.usedfishingtackle.co.uk 2 Brewerton St, HG5 8AZ	01423 865577
York Carp Centre. 2 Oak St, Poppleton Rd, York. YO26 4SE	01904 788856
York Tackle Shop. 31 Yarburgh Way, York. YO10 5HD	01904 411210

I N D E X

NORTH YORKSHIRE VENUES

If you know of a fishery that is not included in this guide or you want to update an existing venue. Please fill in the form below.

Fishery Name

Fishery Address

Post code

Contact Name

Telephone No

Adult Day Ticket Price £   concession OAP'S £

Fish species and approximate weights

Brief Description

Rules / Bans

Facilities

Number of Lakes

Please e-mail or post a colour photo for inclusion in the next publication.

Please return this form to:
Arc Publishing
166 Knowle Lane,
Bents Green,
Sheffield S11 9SJ.

New Fishery ☐

Update to Fishery ☐

chris_keeling@tiscali.co.uk

New Fishery / Fishery Update Form

NOTES